Catching a Meal

Paul Bennett

RSVP

RAINTREE
STECK-VAUGHN
PUBLISHERS
The Steck-Vaughn Company

Austin, Texas

Nature's Secrets

Catching a Meal
Changing Shape
Hibernation
Making a Nest
Migration
Pollinating a Flower

Cover: A male archer fish catches his prey by leaping out of the water. Sometimes archer fish spit at flies or other insects so that they fall into the water.
Title page: A cheetah chases a gazelle.
Contents page: A strand of silk with a blob of glue on the end dangles from a bolas spider.

U.K. copyright © 1994 Wayland (Publishers) Ltd.

U.S. copyright © 1994 Thomson Learning

This edition published by Raintree Steck-Vaughn Publishers, an imprint of Steck-Vaughn Company

Library of Congress Cataloging-in-Publication Data
Bennett, Paul, 1954–
  Catching a meal / Paul Bennett.
       p.   cm.—(Nature's secrets)
  Includes bibliographical references (p.   ) and index.
  ISBN 0-8172-5252-5
  1. Animals—Food—Juvenile literature.
[1. Animals—Food habits.] I. Title. II. Series:
Bennett, Paul, 1954–   Nature's secrets.
QL756.5.B45   1994
591.53—dc20   94-12201

Printed in Italy. Bound in the United States.
2 3 4 5 6 7 8 9 0 02 01 00 99 98

Picture acknowledgments
The publishers would like to thank the following for allowing their photographs to be reproduced in this book: Bruce Coleman Ltd. *cover* (Kim Taylor), 4 (below/Kim Taylor), 5 (above/Frank Greenaway, below/Kim Taylor), 7 (top/Gunter Ziesler), 13 (Kim Taylor), 16 (Kim Taylor), 20 (above/Gerald Cubitt, below/Dr. Frieder Sauer), 21 (above/Dr. Rocco Longo), 23 (main/Felix Labhardt), 28 (Kim Taylor), 29 (above/Kim Taylor, below/John Shaw); Frank Lane Picture Agency 17 (top/Silvestris, below/Eric & David Hosking); the Natural History Photographic Agency *contents page* (A.N.T.), 4 (above/Christophe Ratier), 7 (middle/Stephen Krasemann), 9 (Robert Erwin), 10 (Stephen Dalton), 17 (middle/Silvestris Fotoservice), 21 (below/Anthony Bannister), 22 (above/Stephen Dalton, below/A.N.T.), 27 (above/ Bill Wood); Oxford Scientific Films Ltd. 6 (Waina Cheng), 7 (bottom/Steve Turner), 8 (above/Mary Stouffer Animals Animals, below/David C. Fritts Animals Animals), 11 (below/Frank Huber), 12 (below/Norbert Rosing), 18 (above/Howard Hall), 19 (Tony Tilford), 24 (above/Tom McHugh, below/Howard Hall), 25 (above/Carl Roessler Animals Animals, below/Fred Bavendam), 26 (Fred Bavendam), 27 (below/Colin Milkins); Survival Anglia 11 (above/Jeff Foott), 12 (above/Alan Root), 15 (below Bruce Davidson), 18 (below/Dieter & Mary Plage).

Contents

Introduction

All animals need food to stay alive. Most humans can go shopping for food, but other animals must catch their own meals. Some animals eat only plants, some can also eat meat; but carnivores are unable to digest plants, so they must eat meat. But meat is not an easy meal when you have to catch it first!

◁ This cheetah is chasing a small gazelle. The cheetah can run as fast as 60 mph, but only for about 300 yards or so. If it has not caught its prey within that distance, it has to give up.

An earthworm makes a tasty mouthful for this song thrush. The thrush pulled the worm quickly out of the ground using its slim bill. ▷

4

△ Many frogs like to catch and eat insects. This common frog catches a meal by shooting out its tongue.

Some plants do not get the food they need from the soil, and so they must catch animals too. This large bladderwort has caught a mosquito larva. ▷

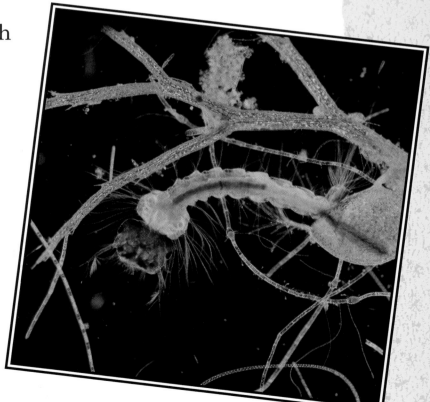

Mammals

Animals hunt either alone or together in packs to help them catch larger prey. Lions use many different methods of hunting, but it is usually a lioness who makes the kill.

△ A lion and lioness stealthily approach their prey so that they can get close enough to leap on it.

△ They have been spotted by the zebra, which runs away. The lioness immediately gives chase.

She has caught the ▷ zebra. The rest of the pride (the group of lions) arrives quickly to help kill the zebra.

Lions, like other flesh-eating mammals, have long, pointed canine teeth for biting their prey. ▷

△ The agile bobcat likes to eat birds and small animals, but it can bring down a deer by leaping onto its back. Here it is chasing a snowshoe hare.

Large, lumbering bears are not swift enough to catch deer. Instead they eat roots, berries, and small animals. Most, like this brown bear, love to eat fish. They stand in the water and wait for some tasty fish to swim by. ▷

△ Stoats are fearsome hunters. They are very agile and can catch and kill animals larger than themselves, such as this rabbit. Stoats are a type of weasel. This stoat has changed from its brown summer coat to white, so that it is camouflaged in the snow.

◁ Many bats emit high-pitched bursts of sound that echo or bounce back to them from objects around them. This is called echolocation. This greater horseshoe bat is swooping to catch a juicy moth by using echolocation.

Otters have powerful tails and webbed feet for swimming swiftly after fish. Sea otters like to dive for shellfish, which they skillfully crack open on a small rock balanced on their stomachs. ▷

A Steller's sea lion enjoys a meal of salmon. Sea lions have strong flippers to enable them to swim as fast as the fish they hunt. This fish came from the ◁ zookeeper.

Reptiles and amphibians

Tortoises, crocodiles, and snakes are all reptiles. Amphibians include frogs, newts, toads, and salamanders. Many of these creatures swim well and are fierce hunters.

◁ A crocodile lies in wait for animals to come down to the water to drink.

It has fearsome teeth for seizing its prey. ▽

A giant chameleon catches an unlucky
fly. The chameleon has a long tongue
that it shoots out in the blink of an eye.
The tongue has a sticky grasping tip for
catching its prey.

The horned frog from South America
will eat almost anything it can catch.
Its huge mouth allows it to swallow a
mouse whole.

△ Poisonous snakes will kill, paralyze, or blind a victim with their venom (poison). The fangs of this rattlesnake are like hypodermic needles for injecting venom into its victim.

Not all snakes are venomous. Constricting snakes stealthily ambush their prey, throw their coils around it, and squeeze it until it cannot breathe. This African python is starting to swallow a squirrel it has killed. ▷

Birds

A huge number of birds are insect-eaters and have slender bills. Others can kill large prey or fish.

△ A barn owl swoops silently to catch a helpless mouse. The owl has very soft feathers, which allow it to fly almost silently as it hunts its prey in the dark of the night.

The kingfisher perches motionless on a branch until it spots a fish.

△ In a flash, it plunges into the water and takes the fish. ▷

It returns to the branch. It will turn the fish around and swallow it head first. ▷

With their flipper-like "wings," these Galapagos penguins "fly" through a school of fish. ▽

◁ The woodpecker finch extracts fat grubs from under the bark of a tree using a tool such as a cactus spine.

The flamingo has a special bill for filtering foods such as algae, snails, and other tiny animals from the water. It holds its bill in an upside-down position. ▷

Insects and spiders

Insects and spiders use all kinds of ways to catch a meal, including chasing, traps, webs, and pouncing.

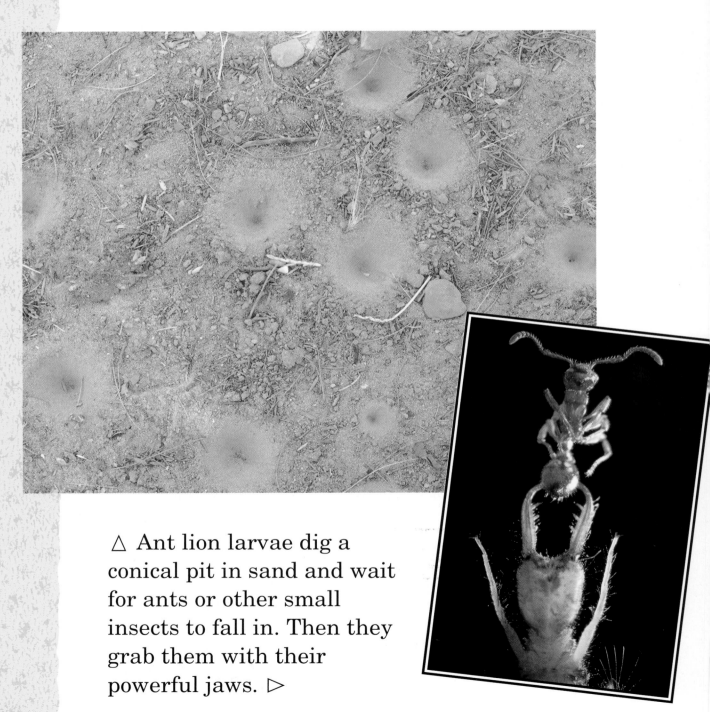

△ Ant lion larvae dig a conical pit in sand and wait for ants or other small insects to fall in. Then they grab them with their powerful jaws. ▷

△ The praying mantis attacks other insects as well as spiders. It holds its arms raised as if praying before pouncing on its victim.

Brightly colored ladybugs feast on juicy aphids. The ladybugs' coloring warns birds that they are not good to eat. ▷

△ A jumping spider leaps on a fly.

◁ A net-casting spider will catch any small insect that passes below with its small web.

The delicate web of a garden spider will trap flying insects. (*Inset*) A strand of silk with a blob of glue on the end dangles from a bolas spider. The spider hopes to catch a moth with it. ▷

Fish and sea creatures

The smell of blood in the water will attract hungry sharks from all directions. This black-tip reef shark is feeding on a mackerel. ▽

◁ Not all sharks are dangerous to people. A basking shark glides through the water with its huge mouth open to catch tiny plankton.

△ A cleaner wrasse "cleans" a bright red bigeye fish by eating parasites.

Like a fisherman, an angler fish uses its worm-shaped lure to attract prey. When the prey comes near, the camouflaged angler fish snaps it up in its huge mouth. ▷

Octopuses are active hunters. The octopus grabs the prey with its tentacles and kills it with a bite from its deadly beak. This Pacific giant octopus is feeding on a dead dogfish shark.

△ Corals with vivid yellow stinging tentacles around the mouth have stunned a fish that has come too close.

Some creatures catch a meal by filtering particles of food from water. An orbshell cockle uses its delicate tubelike siphon to draw in food. ▷

Plants

Some plants that live on poor soil find nourishment by catching small insects.

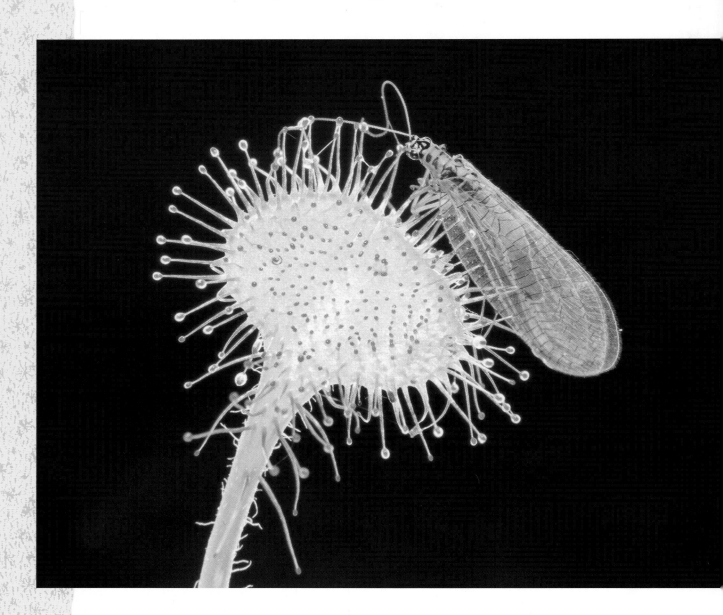

△ The sundew has leaves with sticky "hairs," which trap the insects that land on them. The leaf closes over the insect as it is digested.

△ A dazzling damselfly is about to trigger the leaf of a Venus's-flytrap. Once the leaf closes, the insect cannot escape.

The tubelike leaves of the pitcher plant collect rainwater. A sweet smell from the leaves attracts insects, which slide helplessly down the tube and drown. ▷

29

Glossary

Algae A group of plants that can live in water.

Amphibians Animals that are adapted to live on land and in water.

Camouflaged An animal that is disguised so that it is not easily seen against its background.

Canine One of the four pointed teeth. One is on each side of the upper and lower jaws.

Carnivores Meat-eating animals or plants.

Digest To break up food and turn it into a form that the body can use.

Emit To give out.

Extract To pull out.

Hypodermic needle Fine, hollow needle for giving injections into the skin.

Insect Any small, six-legged creature with a body divided into sections and usually with wings.

Lure Something that attracts; bait.

Mammals Animals whose females give birth to live young, which they feed with milk from their bodies.

Packs Groups of animals of the same kind.

Paralyze To make helpless; results in loss of movement and feeling.

Parasites Animals that live on and obtain nourishment from other animals.

Plankton Very tiny creatures (including animals and plants) that float in the sea.

Prey Animals killed by others for food.

Reptiles Animals, such as lizards, snakes, or turtles, that have a backbone and a scaly skin. They are cold-blooded and usually fully adapted to living on land.

Siphon A tube for drawing off something.

Books to read

Bailey, Donna. *Snakes*. Animal World. Milwaukee: Raintree Steck-Vaughn, 1990.

Bailey, Donna. *Spiders*. Animal World. Milwaukee: Raintree Steck-Vaughn, 1992.

Baskin-Salzberg, Anita and Salzberg, Allen. *Predators!* First Books. New York: Franklin Watts, 1991.

Meadway, Wendy. *Let's Look at Birds*. Let's Look At. New York: Bookwright Press, 1990.

Milkins, Colin S. *Fish*. Weird and Wonderful. New York: Thomson Learning, 1993.

Nielsen, Nancy J. *Carnivorous Plants*. First Books. New York: Franklin Watts, 1992.

Riley, Helen. *Frogs & Toads*. Weird and Wonderful. New York: Thomson Learning, 1993.

Smith, David. *The Food Cycle*. Natural Cycles. New York: Thomson Learning, 1993.

Projects

Project: **Catching Food**

Keep a diary of any animals you observe catching their food. Look for orb spiders' webs in and around your yard. These sticky webs are ideal for catching flying insects. Keep a note of the number of insects that are caught in a day. Name any insects that you recognize.

Some wild animals are used to living near people. You may be lucky to see these animals more clearly by putting food out for them. High in the sky you may see birds of prey hunting for food. If you live near the coast, you may see seabirds diving for fish. Domestic cats sometimes use their hunting instincts to catch small birds and mice. Make a note of your observations.

Project: **Crabs and Anemones**

Crabs and sea anemones catch their food in very different ways. You can set up a temporary aquarium to observe how they feed. Cover the bottom of the aquarium with gravel and put in a pile of rocks so that the crabs can climb out of the water. Fill the aquarium about two-thirds full with seawater, or use artificial seawater from an aquarium supply store. You will also need an air pump.

Visit your local beach and catch a few crabs with a net. Find a small rock or seashell that has sea anemones growing on it. Avoid touching the tentacles: sea anemones sting their prey. Place them in the aquarium. Carefully drop some food into the anemones' tentacles and watch how they feed. Watch the crabs use their claws and mouth parts for eating. Keep a diary of your observations. If you do not live near the coast you could set up an aquarium for freshwater crayfish and other freshwater life.

Places to visit: You may see some of the animals from this book in a zoo, aquarium, or nature park.

Index